Early Maths
Simple Division

Division means to break up a number into equal number of parts.

For example:

If there are 10 apples and you divide them into groups of 5, there will 2 apples in each group.

10 divided by 5 = ?

So, 10 ÷ 5 = 2

In Maths, division is denoted by '÷'. The '/' is also used.

Example:

Divide into groups of 2:

Total items		Items in each group		Number of groups
8	÷	2	=	4

Here are some more examples.

1. Divide into group of 2:

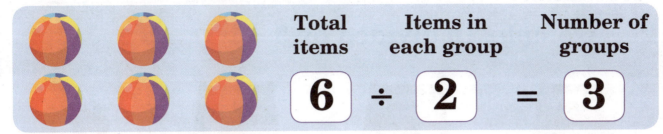

Total items	Items in each group	Number of groups
6 ÷	**2** =	**3**

2. Divide into group of 3:

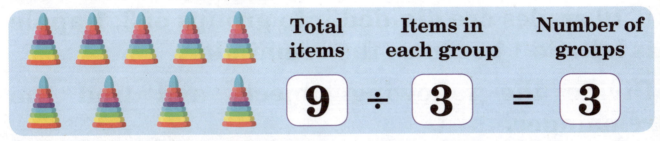

Total items	Items in each group	Number of groups
9 ÷	**3** =	**3**

3. Divide into group of 3:

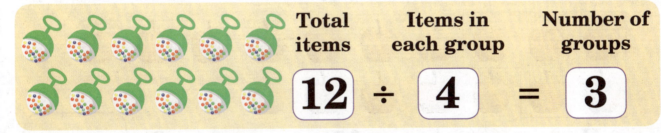

Total items	Items in each group	Number of groups
12 ÷	**4** =	**3**

4. Divide into group of 5:

Total items	Items in each group	Number of groups
10 ÷	**2** =	**5**

5. Divide into group of 4:

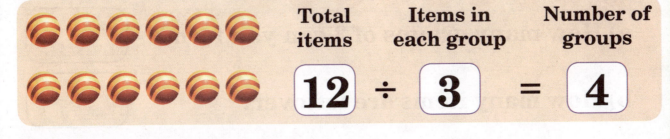

Total items	Items in each group	Number of groups
12 ÷	**3** =	**4**

If a number cannot be divided into equal number of parts, the leftover number is called a **remainder**.

For example, 10 divided by 3 = ?

If 10 apples are divided into groups of 3, 1 apple is left. So 1 becomes the remainder.

Divide the following objects and find the remainder.

1. Divide into groups of 5:

a) How many groups of 5 can you form?

b) How many items are leftover?

2. Divide into groups of 3:

a) How many groups of 3 can you form?

b) How many items are leftover?

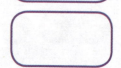

3. Divide into groups of 7:

a) How many groups of 7 can you form?

b) How many items are leftover?

4. Divide into group of 4:

a) How many groups of 4 can you form?

b) How many items are leftover?

5. Divide into groups of 2:

a) How many groups of 2 can you form?

b) How many items are leftover?

5

Objects can be divided into groups in more than one way. Complete the table by finding out number of groups and items leftover.

Total number of apples:

Number of apples in each group	Number of groups	Leftover
6		
3		
9		
11		
7		
13		
4		
8		
14		
15		

7

Look at the group of objects and write the correct division sentence that represents it.

Write division sentence according to the example.

Example:

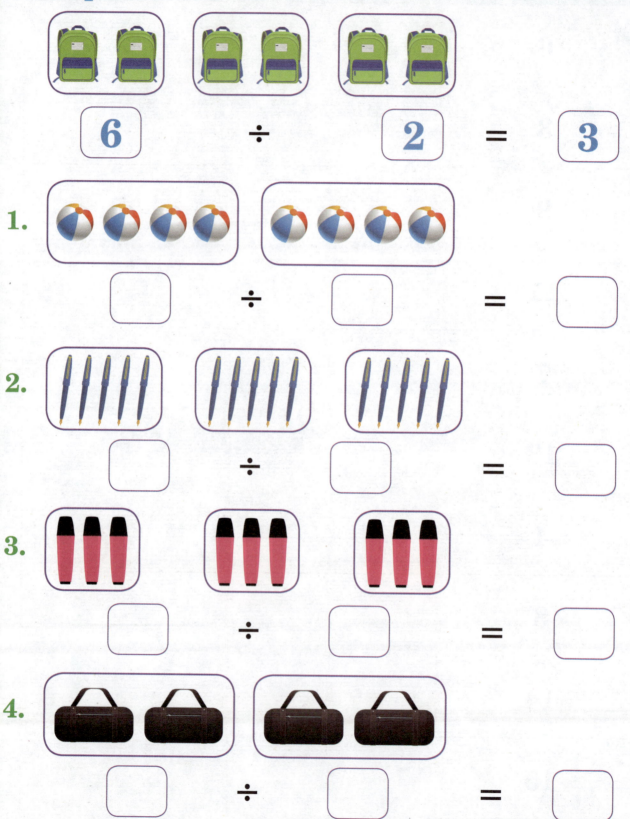

$$6 \div 2 = 3$$

1.

$$\boxed{} \div \boxed{} = \boxed{}$$

2.

$$\boxed{} \div \boxed{} = \boxed{}$$

3.

$$\boxed{} \div \boxed{} = \boxed{}$$

4.

$$\boxed{} \div \boxed{} = \boxed{}$$

5.

$$\boxed{} \div \boxed{} = \boxed{}$$

6.

$$\boxed{} \div \boxed{} = \boxed{}$$

7.

$$\boxed{} \div \boxed{} = \boxed{}$$

8.

$$\boxed{} \div \boxed{} = \boxed{}$$

9.

$$\boxed{} \div \boxed{} = \boxed{}$$

10.

$$\boxed{} \div \boxed{} = \boxed{}$$

The dividend, divisor and quotient are 3 important parts of division.

Dividend ÷ Divisor = Quotient

The dividend is the number you are dividing up.
The divisor is the number you are dividing by.
The quotient is the answer.

Let us look at an example.
$10 ÷ 5 = 2$

Here, 10 is the dividend, that is, the number you are dividing.

5 is the divisor, that is, the number you are dividing the dividend by.

2 is the quotient, that is, the answer.

Remainder Dividend Divisor Quotient

Division is the Opposite of Multiplication

$10 \div 5 = 2$

Replace the = with a x sign and the ÷ with = sign:

$5 \times 2 = 10$

You can also check if your answer is correct using this method.

Some more examples:

$12 \div 3 = 4$

$3 \times 4 = 12$

$72 \div 8 = 9$

$8 \times 9 = 72$

$25 \div 5 = 5$

$5 \times 5 = 25$

Solve the following division problems and find the quotient.

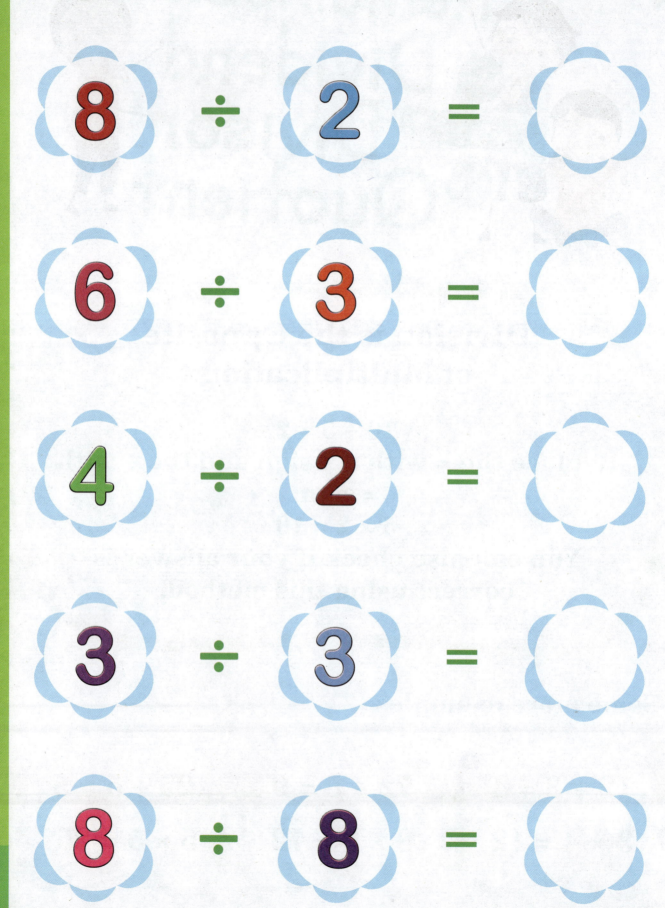

$$8 \div 2 =$$

$$6 \div 3 =$$

$$4 \div 2 =$$

$$3 \div 3 =$$

$$8 \div 8 =$$

$$16 \div 2 = $$

$$15 \div 3 = $$

$$27 \div 3 = $$

$$6 \div 1 = $$

$$4 \div 1 = $$

$$24 \div 3 = $$

Solve some more division problems.

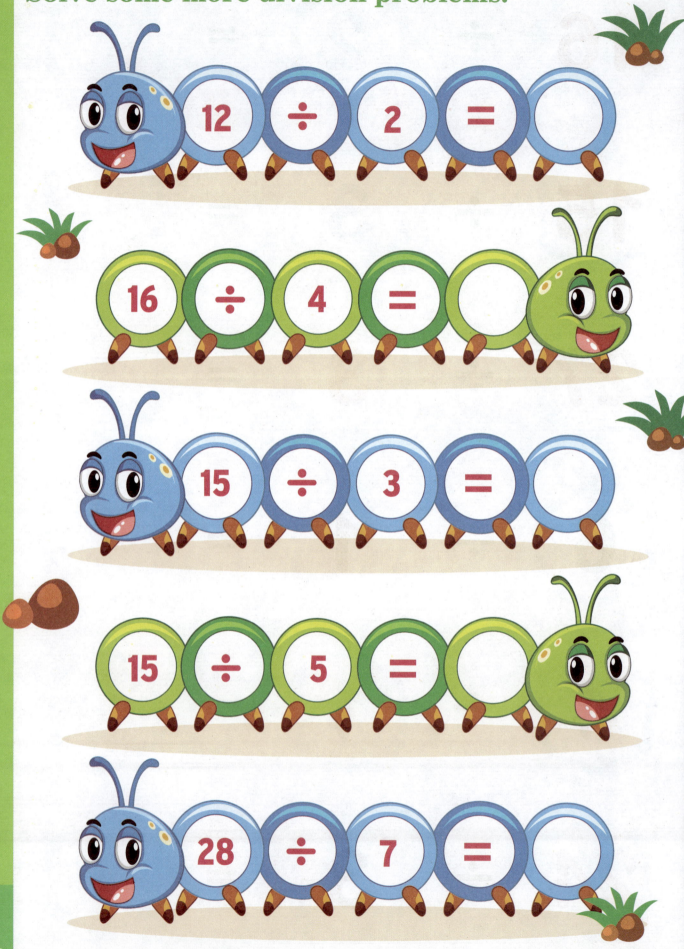

$12 \div 2 = \bigcirc$

$16 \div 4 = \bigcirc$

$15 \div 3 = \bigcirc$

$15 \div 5 = \bigcirc$

$28 \div 7 = \bigcirc$

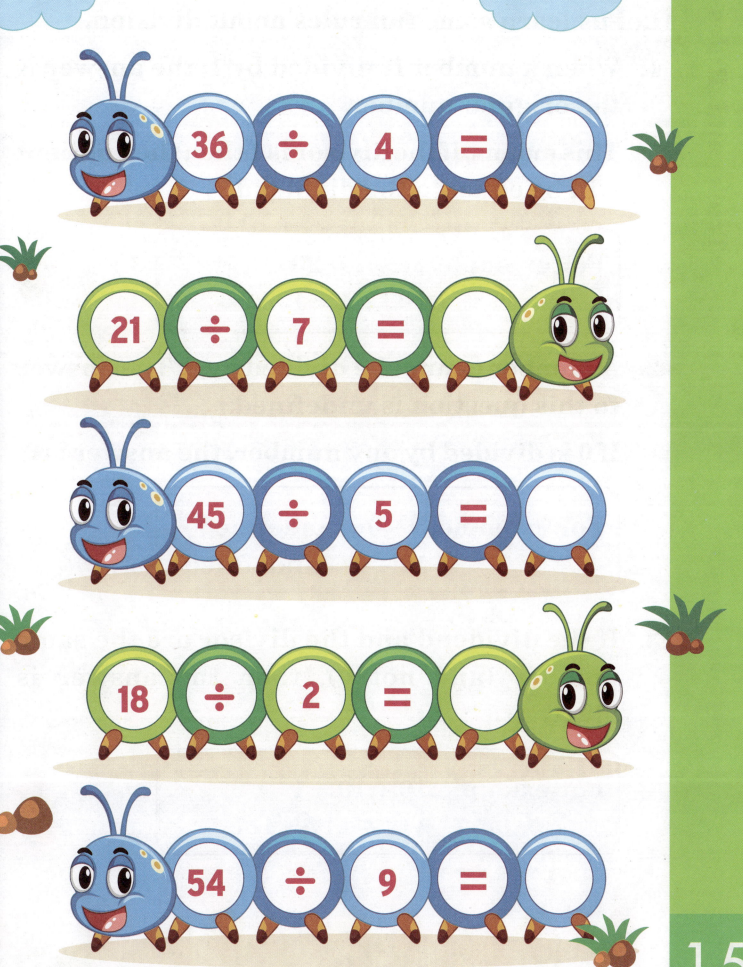

$36 \div 4 =$

$21 \div 7 =$

$45 \div 5 =$

$18 \div 2 =$

$54 \div 9 =$

15

Let us learn some fun rules about division.

1. **When a number is divided by 1, the answer is the original number.**

   This means, if the divisor is 1 then the quotient will be equal to the dividend.

   > For example: $20 \div 1 = 20$
   >
   > $108 \div 1 = 108$

2. **A number cannot be divided by 0. The answer to this question is undefined.**

   If 0 is divided by any number, the answer is 0.

   > For example: $5 \div 0 =$ **undefined**
   >
   > $12 \div 0 =$ **undefined**

3. **If the dividend and the divisor are the same number (and not 0), then the answer is always 1.**

   > For example: $10 \div 10 = 1$
   >
   > $117 \div 117 = 1$

Now solve the following problems based on the given rules.

 2 ÷ 1 =

8 ÷ 1 =

9 ÷ 1 =

0 ÷ 1 =

4 ÷ 1 =

3 ÷ 3 =

15 ÷ 0 =

Divide the objects into groups and write the answer.

1. Divide the 8 umbrellas into groups of 2.

How many groups? _____ $8 \div 2 =$ ☐

2. Divide the 4 fishes into groups 2.

How many groups?_____ $4 \div 2 =$ ☐

3. Divide the 6 ice cream into groups 3.

How many groups?_____ $6 \div 3 =$ ☐

4. Divide the 10 candies into groups 5.

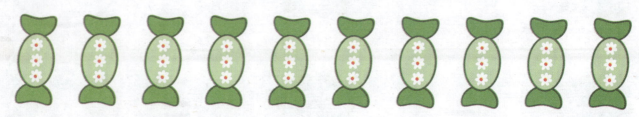

How many groups?_____ $10 \div 5 =$ ☐

5. Divide the 2 cars into groups of 1.

How many groups? _____ $2 \div 1 =$ ☐

6. Divide the 10 boats into groups 2.

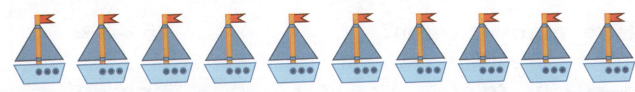

How many groups?_____ $10 \div 2 =$ ☐

7. Divide the 12 rockets into groups 4.

How many groups?_____ $12 \div 4 =$ ☐

8. Divide the 12 airplanes into groups 6.

How many groups?_____ $12 \div 6 =$ ☐

8. Divide the 12 gift box into groups 6.

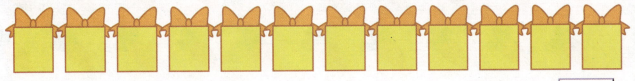

How many groups?_____ $12 \div 6 =$ ☐

How many groups can the objects be divided into?

1. Divide 15 tomatoes into groups of 3.

How many groups?_____ $15 \div 3 =$ ☐

2. Divide 12 pumpkins into groups of 3.

How many groups?_____ $12 \div 3 =$ ☐

3. Divide 14 grape bunches into groups of 2.

How many groups?_____ $14 \div 2 =$ ☐

4. Divide 20 carrots into groups of 5.

How many groups?_____ $20 \div 5 =$ ☐

5. Divide 18 mushrooms into groups of 6.

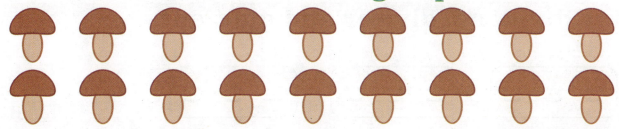

How many groups?_____ $18 \div 6 = \boxed{}$

6. Divide 16 sunflowers into groups of 8.

How many groups?_____ $16 \div 8 = \boxed{}$

7. Divide 24 strawberries into groups of 12.

How many groups?_____ $24 \div 12 = \boxed{}$

8. Divide 12 pineapples into groups of 2.

How many groups?_____ $12 \div 2 = \boxed{}$

Find the number of objects in one group. Write the dividend, divisor and quotient.

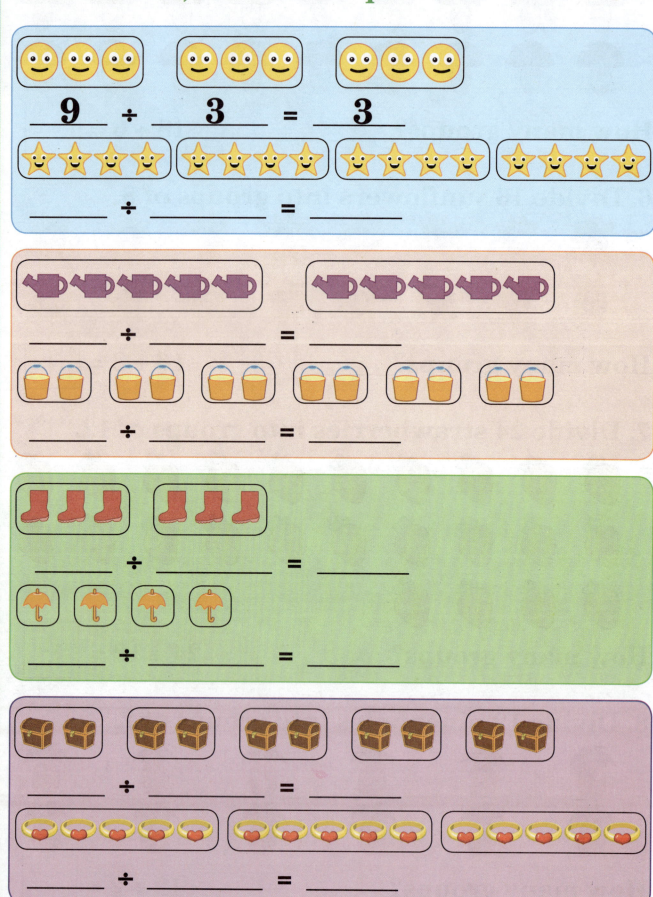

___9___ ÷ ___3___ = ___3___

_____ ÷ _____ = _____

_____ ÷ _____ = _____

_____ ÷ _____ = _____

_____ ÷ _____ = _____

_____ ÷ _____ = _____

_____ ÷ _____ = _____

_____ ÷ _____ = _____

22

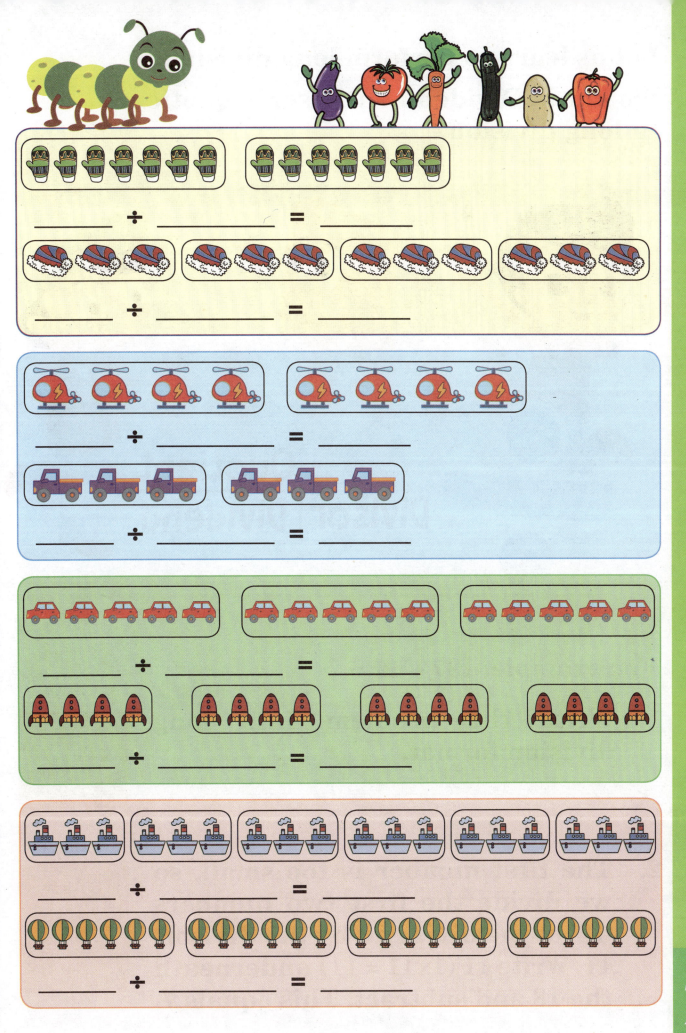

_____ ÷ _____ = _____

_____ ÷ _____ = _____

_____ ÷ _____ = _____

_____ ÷ _____ = _____

_____ ÷ _____ = _____

_____ ÷ _____ = _____

_____ ÷ _____ = _____

_____ ÷ _____ = _____

Let us learn to perform long division.

We know, Dividend ÷ Divisor = Quotient

In long division,

$$\text{Divisor} \overline{\smash{\big)}\ \text{Dividend}}^{\text{Quotient}}$$

For example, 187 ÷ 11 = ?

1. Write the problem into long division format.

$$11 \overline{\smash{\big)}\ 187}$$

2. The first number is too small, so we divide the first two numbers '18' of the dividend by the divisor, 11. Write 11 (1x11 = 11) underneath the 18 and subtract. This equals 7.

$$\begin{array}{r} 1 \\ 11 \overline{\smash{\big)}\ 187} \\ \underline{11} \\ 7 \end{array}$$

3. Now move the next number (7) down from the end of the 187.

4. How many times 11, will divide into 77? Write 7 next to the 1 in the quotient. We also write down 77 underneath the 77 because 7 x 11 = 77.

5. Now subtract. The answer is zero. So, 187 ÷ 11 = 17.

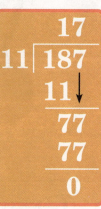

Some more examples of long division are:

25

Count the total number of objects and circle the equal groups. Write the division sentence and the long division format. Follow the example.

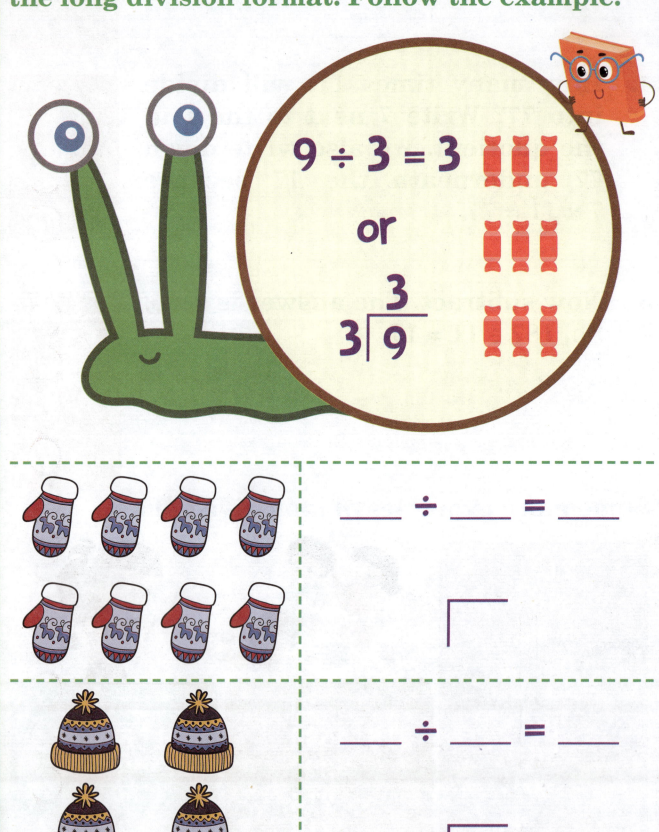

$9 \div 3 = 3$

or

$$3 \overline{)9}$$ with quotient 3

___ ÷ ___ = ___

___ ÷ ___ = ___

26

$$\underline{\hspace{2cm}} \div \underline{\hspace{2cm}} = \underline{\hspace{2cm}}$$

$$\underline{\hspace{2cm}} \div \underline{\hspace{2cm}} = \underline{\hspace{2cm}}$$

$$\underline{\hspace{2cm}} \div \underline{\hspace{2cm}} = \underline{\hspace{2cm}}$$

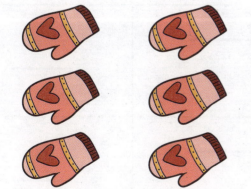

$$\underline{\hspace{2cm}} \div \underline{\hspace{2cm}} = \underline{\hspace{2cm}}$$

Write the different ways in which a division problem can be written. Also, find the answer.

$29 \div 8 = \underline{}$	$8\overline{)29}$	$\dfrac{29}{8}$
$37 \div 9 = \underline{}$	$\overline{)}$	$\underline{}$
$25 \div 7 = \underline{}$	$\overline{)}$	$\underline{}$
$21 \div 6 = \underline{}$	$\overline{)}$	$\underline{}$
$47 \div 5 = \underline{}$	$\overline{)}$	$\underline{}$
$59 \div 4 = \underline{}$	$\overline{)}$	$\underline{}$
$46 \div 7 = \underline{}$	$\overline{)}$	$\underline{}$
$28 \div 9 = \underline{}$	$\overline{)}$	$\underline{}$

28

32 ÷ 8 = _____	8 $\overline{)32}$	$\dfrac{32}{8}$
48 ÷ 6 = _____	$\overline{}$	_____
16 ÷ 2 = _____	$\overline{}$	_____
21 ÷ 3 = _____	$\overline{}$	_____
35 ÷ 5 = _____	$\overline{}$	_____
21 ÷ 7 = _____	$\overline{}$	_____
18 ÷ 6 = _____	$\overline{}$	_____
10 ÷ 5 = _____	$\overline{}$	_____

Solve the problems using the long division method.

$2\overline{)18}$

$3\overline{)24}$

$4\overline{)32}$

$2\overline{)12}$

$3\overline{)27}$

$4\overline{)28}$

$2\overline{)14}$

$3\overline{)18}$

$4\overline{)36}$

$5\overline{)40}$

$6\overline{)48}$

$7\overline{)49}$

$5\overline{)30}$

$8\overline{)56}$

$7\overline{)63}$

$9\overline{)72}$

$8\overline{)72}$

$7\overline{)56}$

Use the long division method and find the quotient.

$$2\overline{)248}$$

$$2\overline{)284}$$

$$2\overline{)482}$$

$$2\overline{)428}$$

$$2\overline{)824}$$

$$2\overline{)842}$$

$$2\overline{)484}$$

$$2\overline{)284}$$

$$2\overline{)828}$$

$9\overline{)414}$

$3\overline{)612}$

$7\overline{)987}$

$2\overline{)806}$

$5\overline{)725}$

$6\overline{)402}$

$7\overline{)819}$

$4\overline{)936}$

$5\overline{)700}$

The following division problems have a remainder. Solve them using the long division method.

$$3\overline{)76}$$

$$8\overline{)99}$$

$$7\overline{)46}$$

$$3\overline{)41}$$

$$3\overline{)53}$$

$$2\overline{)69}$$

$4\overline{)31}$

$5\overline{)12}$

$6\overline{)70}$

$9\overline{)77}$

$7\overline{)55}$

$4\overline{)41}$

Solve the following using the long division method.

$3\overline{)42}$

$7\overline{)56}$

$8\overline{)16}$

$2\overline{)98}$

$7\overline{)84}$

$3\overline{)75}$

$$4 \overline{)48}$$

$$7 \overline{)81}$$

$$6 \overline{)72}$$

$$5 \overline{)65}$$

$$9 \overline{)27}$$

$$2 \overline{)36}$$

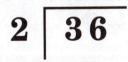

Find the quotient and the remainder (if any).

$7\overline{)52}$

$9\overline{)81}$

$8\overline{)64}$

$5\overline{)13}$

$4\overline{)96}$

$6\overline{)28}$

$3\overline{)49}$

$4\overline{)78}$

$9\overline{)98}$

$2\overline{)60}$

$8\overline{)73}$

$3\overline{)56}$

$5\overline{)15}$

$6\overline{)32}$

$4\overline{)20}$

$3\overline{)86}$

$9\overline{)42}$

$8\overline{)53}$

Solve the division word problems.

4 friends go to the local farm to pluck apples. They pick 40 apples in total. How many apples will each one get if they divide it equally among all?

40 apples have to be divided among 4 friends.

So, 40 ÷ 4 = _____

A teacher distributes 27 crayons equally among 9 children in the class. How many crayons will each child receive?

Lily baked 18 chocolate chip cookies for her children and their friends. If she distributes the cookies among 6 children equally, then how many cookies will each child get?

_____

32 sunflowers are planted on all sides of a square garden. If all the sides have the same number of flowers, how many sunflowers are there on one side?

_____

Claire goes to the florist to buy 100 roses. The florist divides them equally in 5 bouquets. How many flowers are there in each bouquet?

Holly has 36 pairs of shoes in total. If they are arranged equally in 4 shelves, how many shoes can be found in each shelf?

_____ ÷ _____ = _____ **shoes**

A classroom has a total of 21 benches. If they are arranged in 3 rows, how many benches can be found in each row?

_____ ÷ _____ = _____ **benches**

Kate made 45 Popsicles for 5 of her cousins. How many Popsicles did she make for each cousin?

_____ ÷ _____ = _____ **Popsicles**

A baker baked a total of 78 éclairs for a birthday party. If all the éclairs are arranged in 6 plates, how many éclairs are there in each plate?

_____ ÷ _____ = _____ éclairs

There are 12 butterflies near 6 flowers in the garden. If there are same number of butterflies on each flower, how many butterflies are there on one flower?

_____ ÷ _____ = _____ butterflies

65 ounces of juice is poured equally into 6 glasses from a pitcher. How many ounces of juice does each glass contain? Also calculate how many ounces of juice remains in the pitcher?

Each glass contains _____ ounces of juice.

_____ of juice is left in the pitcher.

In a toy factory, 71 toys need to be packed in equal numbers in 3 cartons. How many toys will be packed in each carton? How many toys will be left after all the toys have been divided and packed equally?

____ toys will be packed in each carton. ____ toys will remain after all the toys have been divided and packed equally.

Jenny has 58 candy bars which she distributes equally among her 5 cousins. How many candy bars does each cousin get? Are there any candy bars left with Jenny? If yes, then write how many.

Each cousin gets ____ candy bars. ____ candy bars are left.

Bella's mother has made 38 sandwiches for her class picnic. Each lunch box can only contain 4 sandwiches. How many lunchboxes will be used? What is the remaining number of sandwiches?

____ lunch boxes will be used. ____ sandwiches remain.

Find the quotient by solving the following using long division.

5) 755	6) 966	7) 959

8) 996	5) 935	6) 864

7) 945	8) 944	9) 999

$$3 \overline{)996}$$

$$3 \overline{)969}$$

$$3 \overline{)993}$$

$$4 \overline{)484}$$

$$4 \overline{)844}$$

$$2 \overline{)862}$$

$$2 \overline{)448}$$

$$2 \overline{)844}$$

$$2 \overline{)228}$$

There are 94 colourful baubles available to decorate 6 Christmas trees. If equal number of baubles are used to decorate the trees, how many are used to decorate one tree? What is the number of baubles that were not decorated on any tree?

_____

_____

A supermarket has 83 shopping baskets that need to be arranged equally in 5 stacks. How many shopping baskets were arranged in each stack? What is the remaining number of baskets that were not stacked?

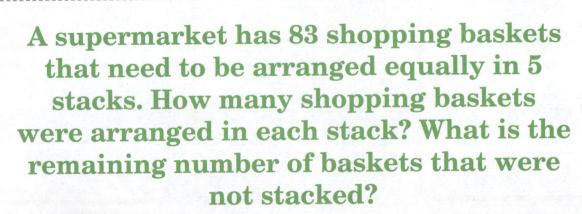

_____

_____

Stacy and 5 of her friends ordered 2 large pizzas of 8 slices each. If the slices were divided equally among the friends, how many slices did each one eat? How many sluices were left for Stacy to eat?

_____

_____

Elsa has space for just 57 pieces of clothing in her closet. They have to be divided equally among 4 drawers in her cupboard. How many clothes fit in each drawer? How many pieces of clothes could not fit in her cupboard?

_____

_____

A new office has employed 67 persons. If 3 members share a cabin, how many cabins are required to accommodate everyone? What is the remaining number of persons without a cabin?

_____

_____

Jason has 38 photo frames that need to be spread equally across 3 rooms of his house. How many photo frames were put up in each of the 3 rooms? What is the number of the remaining frames?

_____

_____

There are 85 logs of firewood in the garage. If they are arranged equally in 8 bundles, how many logs are there in each bundle? What is the remaining number of firewood that are not stacked?

_____

_____

A recipe requires 810 mangoes to prepare 80 bottles of jam. If equal number of mangoes are used to prepare one bottle of jam, how many mangoes are required to make one bottle? What is the remaining number of mangoes?

_____

_____

Look at the given picture. Answer the questions based on the picture.

1. Two friends visited a local supermarket. They picked a bag of oranges for $18 and decided to share them equally. How much money will each friend have to pay?

    _____

2. The shampoo aisle in the supermarket includes 50 shampoo bottles arranged in 5 rows. How many shampoo bottles can be found in each row?

    _____

3. They bought 4 packets of chocolates. What is the cost of each packet if they were billed $44 in total for the chocolates?

_____

4. A single door display refrigerator at the supermarket can hold 81 beverages. If the refrigerator has 9 racks in total, how many beverages will be there in each rack?

_____

5. There are 4 cash counters at the store. 20 customers are waiting to pay their bills. Equal number of customers are standing at the counters to pay their bills. How many customers are standing at each cash counter?

_____

6. In the parking lot, there are 55 cars. If the car parking has 10 rows with equal number of parked cars, how many cars are parked in each row? How many cars are not parked?

_____

Answer the questions based on this picture.

1. The school is taking grade 2 students to the museum. The entry fee for the entire class is $250. If there are 25 students in the class, how much fee will each student pay?

_____

2. The school is hosting an inter-school basketball competition for grade 5. Each team will have 6 students each. If there are 48 students in total, how many teams will be formed?

_____

3. Patrick is a student of grade 3 and it is his birthday. He brought 15 muffins to share with 6 of his friends. If he divides the muffins equally among 6 of his friends, how many muffins does each friend eat? How many muffins are left for Patrick to eat?

---

4. Grade 4 has a total number of 28 students. If the classroom has 7 rows in total, how many students are seated in each row?

---

5. Jane, a student of grade 4 brings a box of 35 pencils to the school on Monday. She wants to split them equally among 4 of her friends. How many pencils will each of them receive? How many pencils are left for Jane?

---

6. There are a total of 247 students in school. Some students travel by bus, other walk home. If there are 5 buses that carry equal number of students, how many students travel in each bus? How many students do not travel by bus?

1. A waiter works 8 hour shifts at a restaurant. If he earns $448 per week, what will be his daily wage?

_____

2. A parking lot has 252 parking spaces. If each row has space for 3 cars, how many rows are there in the parking lot?

_____

3. A family of three checked in at a hotel for a 6-day stay. If they were charged $882 per person for the 6-day stay, what is the average cost per person per day?

_____

4. A shop sold 990 pine tree during a five day Christmas sale. What is the average number of pumpkins sold in one day?

_____

5. A snow plough uses 144 litres of diesel over a three-day period to clear up the roads. How many gallons of diesel was used up on an average in one day?

_____

6. Gale baked a 5 tier cake for her niece's birthday party. She decorated it with 300 strawberries. If there are same number of strawberries on each tier, find out the average number of strawberries on each tier.

_____

1. Aaron, a professional photographer clicked 848 photos at his friend's wedding reception. He arranged them equally in 8 separate folders on his computer. How many wedding photos does each folder contain?

_____

2. Lillian counted 426 apple trees in her grandfather's orchard. If the trees are planted in six rows in the orchard, what is the average number of trees in each row?

3. John purchased a bag of dry food for his pet dog. It contains approximately 198 cups of dry food. If the dog consumes an average of 3 bowls a day, how many days will the bag of dry food last?

4. If a team of 6 players shoot 168 hoops while playing basketball, on an average how many hoops does one player shoot?

5. During the heavy festive rush, a post office received 545 packages to be delivered. The packages were divided equally among 5 postmen. How many packages were carried for delivery by each postman?

1. A delivery van travelled a distance of 608 miles. If it used up 19 gallons of fuel for the entire trip, calculate the average miles covered per gallon.

2. Kris bought 10 packs of 300 glossy photo papers. Find out the average number of papers in each pack.

3. A total of 108 students participated in the singing competition. If 12 students were part of each team, how many teams participated in total?

4. Daphne baked 264 cupcakes which were to be delivered for a party. If one box can hold 8 cupcakes, how many boxes will she require to pack all the cupcakes?

5. A store receives 380 cartons of milk. If 19 slots are available to store the cartons, how many milk cartons will be stacked in each slot?

6. A farm-stand produces apple cider that is served in 10-ounce bottles. How many bottles will be required to serve 880 ounces of apple cider?

1. A public library has 1248 reference books arranged in 6 racks equally. How many books does each rack hold?

2. Nathan withdrew $1000 from his account and exchanged the $1000 bill for $100 bills at the local grocer. How many 100-dollar bills did Jeremy receive from the grocer?

3. A parking facility can accommodate up to 4,000 vehicles at a time. If there are 8 levels in the facility, how many vehicles can be parked on each level?

4. Terry is employed as a part-time server at a restaurant. If he earns a total of $2,422 in one month, how much money does he earn in a day?

5. A ski resort is spread over an area of 4,988 acres. The resort is divided equally into 4 major centres. What is the size of each centre?

6. Five churners in a chocolate factory can produce 1000 tons of liquid chocolate in a year. How many tons of liquid chocolate can one churner produce in a year?

7. The room service of a hotel received 92 soiled sheets from 5 floors. If it received equal number of sheets from each floor, how many sheets belong to each floor? How many extra sheets did they receive that did not belong to any floor?

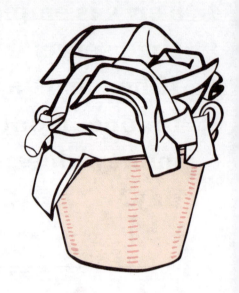

8. Mark buys three crates of oranges. He gives $100 bill to the cashier. How much did each crate cost, if he receives $13 as change?

9. An egg tray can hold 12 eggs each. 104 farm fresh eggs need to be packed. What is the number of trays that will be required to hold 12 eggs each? How many eggs remain to be packed?

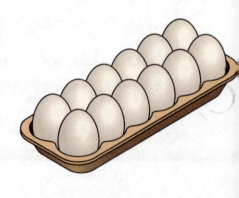